MARTIN LUTHER KING, JR.

Other titles in the
PEOPLE WHO MADE A DIFFERENCE
series include

Marie Curie
Father Damien
Mahatma Gandhi
Bob Geldof
Mother Teresa

North American edition first published in 1990 by
Gareth Stevens Children's Books
1555 North RiverCenter Drive, Suite 201
Milwaukee, Wisconsin 53212, USA

First published in the United Kingdom in 1989. This edition
is abridged from the original published in 1988 by Exley
Publications Ltd. and written by Valerie Schloredt with Pam
Brown. Copyright © 1988 by Exley Publications. Additional
end matter © 1990 by Gareth Stevens, Inc.

For a free color catalog describing
Gareth Stevens' list of high-quality
children's books, call

   1-800-341-3569 (USA) or
   1-800-461-9120 (Canada)

PICTURE CREDITS
All pictures except those listed below
are © Flip Schulke or are from the
Schulke Archives, Florida. The
publishers gratefully acknowledge his
permission to reproduce them.
   BBC Hulton Picture Library — 4
(both); Black Star, New York — Charles
Moore 30 (below), 45 (both); Tom
Redman — cover illustration; Rex
Features — 8, 9; Val Wilmer — 6.
   Map drawn by Geoff Pleasance.
   The publishers have been unable to
identify the owner of the picture of
Gandhi on page 12; any information
that would allow them to do so would
be much appreciated.

The publishers thank Joan Daves for
permission to reprint material copyright
© 1955, 1956, 1963 by Martin Luther
King, Jr.; copyright © 1968 by the
Estate of Martin Luther King, Jr. The
publishers also wish to express their
gratitude to Flip Schulke, King's friend
and photographer, for advice in
preparing the text and for clarifying
points in the story. Without his
assistance, the task of preparing this
book would have been much
more difficult.

Library of Congress Cataloging-in-Publication Data

Birch, Beverley.
   Martin Luther King, Jr.: leader in the struggle for civil rights / by
Valerie Schloredt; this edition written by Beverley Birch. — North
American ed.
      p.   cm.
   Summary: Recounts the life of the Nobel Prize-winning civil rights
leader, Dr. Martin Luther King.
   ISBN 0-8368-0392-2
   1. King, Martin Luther, Jr., 1929-1968—Juvenile literature. 2. Civil
rights workers—United States—Biography—Juvenile literature. 3.
Baptists—United States—Clergy—Biography—Juvenile literature.
4. Afro-Americans—Biography—Juvenile literature. [1. King,
Martin Luther, Jr., 1929-1968. 2. Civil rights workers. 3. Clergy. 4.
Afro-Americans—Biography.] I. Schloredt, Valerie. Martin Luther
King, Jr. II. Title.
E185.97.K5B495   1990   323'.092—dc20
[B]   [92]   89-77587

Series conceived and edited by Helen Exley
Series editors, U.S.: Amy Bauman and Rhoda Irene Sherwood
Additional end matter, U.S.: John D. Rateliff
Cover design: Kate Kriege

Printed in Hungary

       1 2 3 4 5 6 7 8 9 96 95 94 93 92 91 90

PEOPLE
WHO MADE
A DIFFERENCE

Leader in the struggle for civil rights

MARTIN LUTHER KING, JR.

Beverley Birch's adaptation of the book by Valerie Schloredt

Gareth Stevens Children's Books
MILWAUKEE

Above: This photograph of slaves in West Africa was taken in the 1890s. In the United States, slavery was abolished by the Thirteenth Amendment to the Constitution in 1865, but it continued in many parts of the world.

Right: A black woman is sold as a slave in America. King's own grandfather was born a slave.

Slavery

For thousands of people from Europe, America in the 1800s was a land of hope and freedom where they had a chance for a better life. But for the black people of America, it was a different story.

Since the early 1600s, millions of black Africans had been snatched from their homelands and carried across the Atlantic Ocean to America. Here, they were sold into slavery to work on white people's lands and in their homes. Slaves were bought and sold like animals. Husbands were separated from their wives, children from their parents. Slaves had no freedom. They could not choose where they lived or what work they did. They belonged to their owners, who often made them work much too hard. They were not always given enough food. They were often beaten — sometimes to death.

In the beginning of the nineteenth century, some white people began to speak out against slavery. These people believed that it was wrong for one person to own another. The Northern states of America put an end to, or abolished, slavery early in the nineteenth century.

"We have in common with all other men a natural right to our freedoms. . . . But we were unjustly dragged by the cruel hand of power from our dearest friends and some of us stolen from the bosoms of our tender parents . . . and from a . . . pleasant and plentiful country and brought hither to be made slaves for life in a Christian land."
"A Slave Petition for Freedom," 1774

5

After 1865, black people in the United States were "free," but they were still very poor because many had no land. The economic depression of the 1930s hit black people worst of all.

New Jersey was the last Northern state to do this, in 1804. But in the Southern states, slavery continued.

In 1861, eleven of the Southern states broke off from the United States. They formed a separate nation, called the Confederate States of America. The Confederacy wanted slavery to continue, but the Northern states wanted slavery abolished. The American Civil War followed. After four years of fighting, the Northern states won. And slavery was abolished in 1865 by the Thirteenth Amendment to the Constitution.

After the Civil War, America became a rich country. For many people, life became very comfortable. But although African-Americans were no longer slaves, their lives were often terrible. They could not afford to buy land or good houses. They could get only jobs that white people would not do.

Then came the economic depression of the 1930s. It hit black people harder than it hit white people because black people had less to begin with. And so, almost one hundred years after the abolition of slavery, life for many African-Americans was worse than it had been under a system of slavery.

Worse yet were people's attitudes. Many white people still thought that they were better than black people. These people believed that all black people were lazy and stupid. In the Southern states, all black men were called "boy" even if they were old men.

"Jim Crow"

Slavery had been abolished at the end of the Civil War, but the Southern states still made laws that separated black people and white people. This separation was called segregation. The laws and customs that kept segregation in place were called "Jim Crow."

Among other things, the laws said that black people could not eat or drink in the same places as white people. Black people could not go to the same churches as whites. They could not sit in seats saved for white people.

"Among white women who worked, one of ten was employed as a maid; among black women, six of ten were so employed."
Richard Polenberg, in One Nation Divisible: Class, Race and Ethnicity in the U.S. since 1938

"Jim Crow meant more than physical separation. Separate waiting rooms at bus stations, separate railroad cars, separate sections in movie theaters, separate schools and churches, separate restaurants and drinking fountains."
Richard Polenberg, in One Nation Divisible: Class, Race and Ethnicity in the U.S. since 1938

This photograph of members of the Ku Klux Klan was taken in the 1980s. Although the Ku Klux Klan has lost a lot of power in the last thirty years, it is still strong in some Southern and Midwestern states.

The Ku Klux Klan

After the Civil War, some white people in the Southern states started the Ku Klux Klan (KKK). The Klan is a vicious group.

Members of the Ku Klux Klan believe strongly that white people are better than all other races. Klan members believe that black people are the lowest race. They do not want African-Americans to have any power in the United States. They want total segregation of the races.

The Klan has always used fear to get people to do what they want. They wear white clothes with peculiar tall, pointed hoods that hide their faces. These costumes keep their identities a secret. They also make the members look very frightening. Besides this, the Klan holds strange ceremonies in front of burning crosses. Worst of all, they use violence.

From the beginning, many Klan members held important jobs in their towns and villages. For example, many

Opposite: The Ku Klux Klan holds strange ceremonies in front of a burning cross. This is meant to frighten people. From 1900 to 1930, Ku Klux Klan members killed hundreds of black people by hanging, or "lynching," them.

were policemen. They made sure that KKK members were not punished for their crimes. Since the 1950s, there have been fewer killings in the Southern states, but the Klan still harasses black people. In some places — especially some Southern and Midwestern states — the Klan still has many members.

In the years after 1865, brave men and women worked for justice and equality for African-Americans. But even in the 1950s, they had a long way to go. They needed a leader to help them along.

Dr. Martin Luther King became that leader in the 1950s and 1960s. He led African-Americans in a great nonviolent protest. His work changed the attitudes of millions of people in the United States and all over the world.

This was Martin's family home on Auburn Avenue, Atlanta, Georgia, when he was a child. The family had a comfortable life because Martin's father was a banker.

Martin Luther King's childhood

Named after his father, Martin Luther King, Jr., was born on January 15, 1929, in Atlanta, Georgia. His family included his parents, a grandmother, a brother, and a sister. Martin's father was a banker, so the family lived comfortably. "Daddy King," as Martin's father was called, was also the minister at Atlanta's Ebenezer Baptist Church. He was active in the black community.

Although Martin's life in Atlanta was comfortable, he met racism — the belief that one race is better than another —

every day. He could not use certain public toilets, because they were only for white people. If he wanted to buy ice cream, he had to go to a window at the shop's side. If he went to the movies, he had to sit upstairs at the back. He could not go to school with white children. He could not use the same libraries or parks as white people.

When Martin was very young, he had two white friends. One day, the boys' mother suddenly sent Martin home. She told him not to come to her house again. She said that her boys were too old to play with a black child. Martin was very hurt. His parents tried to explain that white people were not better than he was. They told him he was as good as any child, black or white.

Another sad event happened when Martin was fifteen and in high school. He, some classmates, and their teacher went to a school near Atlanta for a speech contest. There, Martin made a speech about the rights of African-Americans, and he won a prize. Both Martin and his teacher were very happy as they rode back to Atlanta on the bus.

But that night, the bus was crowded. At first, Martin and his teacher had seats. But at that time in the South, black people had to stand at the back of the bus if white people wanted their seats. When two white people got on the bus after a

This photograph of some members of the Ku Klux Klan was taken in the 1950s. They were ordinary people and some were even community leaders. Many children were brought up to believe that black people were inferior to white people.

Mahatma Gandhi led India to independence from Great Britain in the 1940s. Throughout his life, Gandhi believed in using peaceful protest. King wanted African-Americans to follow Gandhi's ideas of nonviolent protest. He believed that if they did, they could get equal rights with white people.

few stops, the bus driver made Martin and his teacher stand up. Martin was very angry. But he did as he was told because his teacher was afraid. He said later that that was one of the worst moments of his life.

Lessons from Daddy King

Although Martin's father was important in the black community, most white people thought of him as just another "nigger."* He hated this racism and the laws of segregation. He once said, "I don't care how long I have to live with the system. I am never going to accept it. I'll fight it until I die."

Martin Luther King, Jr., did not forget his father's words. But the elder King's actions impressed his son even more. Martin remembered a time when a policeman stopped his father on the road. "Let me see your driver's license, boy," the policeman said. Martin's father pointed at his son and said, "See that child there? That's a boy. I am a man."

College days

Martin entered college when he was fifteen — three years earlier than most young people begin college. He went to

*Editor's note: Some people of this time referred to African-Americans as "niggers." This was an insult, and it is still not an acceptable term. We use it here only to accurately reflect the attitudes of some whites toward African-Americans.

Morehouse College in Atlanta, one of America's best black colleges of the time. Martin knew that he was lucky. At the time, very few black students got the chance to go to college.

Martin's father wanted his son to become a minister. At first, Martin had other plans. He wanted to help the black community, and he thought he should become a doctor or a lawyer to do it.

The president of Morehouse College at that time was Dr. Benjamin Mays. He believed that the church could do a lot to help African-Americans. After he had listened to Dr. Mays, Martin decided to become a minister after all.

The Ebenezer Baptist Church in Atlanta, Georgia, was Martin's father's church. When he was seventeen, Martin preached his first sermon here. Soon afterward, he was ordained as a Baptist minister. He was assistant minister at the church from 1948 to 1954. In 1959, he went back to Atlanta and was co-minister of the church with his father until his death.

Martin Luther King studied theology at Crozer Theological Seminary in Chester, Pennsylvania, from 1948 to 1951. As one of six black students out of more than one hundred students, King had a difficult time at first. "I'm afraid I was grimly serious for a time. I had a tendency to overdress, to keep my room spotless, my shoes perfectly shined, and my clothes immaculately pressed."

He preached his first sermon at his father's church in Atlanta. He was only seventeen years old, but he preached well. The people who heard him knew that Martin Luther King, Jr., was a good preacher. Soon after this, he was ordained as a minister.

In the summer of 1948, Martin graduated from Morehouse College. But he had not finished studying yet. In the autumn, he went to Crozer Theological Seminary in Chester, Pennsylvania. As one of only six black students, King found life difficult there at first. But he worked hard and did well.

While there, he studied the works of great theologians (people who write about religion) and philosophers (people who write about the meaning of life). He especially liked the ideas of the

American philosopher Henry David Thoreau (1817-1862). Thoreau hated slavery and worked hard to abolish it. In 1846, as a protest against slavery, Thoreau refused to pay his taxes. For his protest, he spent a night in jail.

Martin also liked the ideas of the Indian Mahatma Gandhi (1869-1948). Gandhi had led the people of India in their fight to rule their own country. For many years, India had been ruled by the British government.

Mahatma Gandhi believed in nonviolent protest at all times. He led the Indian people in protests against the British again and again. He told his people that they must be ready to go to jail for their beliefs. He said they must be ready to die for independence but they must never kill for it. Martin began to believe that African-Americans should follow Gandhi's ideas.

Martin meets Coretta

In 1951, King graduated from Crozer Theological Seminary at the top of his class. After that, he continued his studies at Boston University in Massachusetts.

It was in Boston that King met Coretta Scott. Like Martin, she came from the South. But Coretta grew up on a farm in Alabama. On June 18, 1953, they were married by Martin's father at Coretta's home in Marion, Alabama.

King was twenty-five when he took his first minister's position at Dexter Avenue Baptist Church, Montgomery, Alabama. He served the church from September 1954 to November 1959.

Later that year, they both finished their courses in Boston. Martin began to look for a job. He wanted to teach in a university, but he thought that he should work as a minister for a few years first. Besides this, he still had to write a paper, called a dissertation, to get his doctoral degree from Boston University.

Back in the South

King took a job as the minister of Dexter Avenue Baptist Church in Montgomery, Alabama. He and Coretta had talked for a long time before they decided to return to the South. They did not want to go back to the racism and segregation that they knew existed in the South. But with their families still there, the South was still home. They also wanted to try to make things better for Southern black people. And going back was the only way to do that.

And so, in September 1954, Martin and Coretta moved to Montgomery. Martin began work as minister to the Dexter Avenue Baptist Church. The small brick church had been built just after the Civil War. It served only about four hundred people. Still, the Kings had a busy life.

King got up at 5:30 A.M. each morning. This gave him three hours before breakfast to work on his dissertation. After this, he then put in a full day's work at his church. By this time, King

Many of the events in this book took place in the Southern states (shaded tan on this map). Many of these states allowed slavery before the Civil War and fought on the Confederate side in that war. African-Americans make up 12.3 percent of all the people in the United States. In the past, most black people lived in the states of the old Confederacy. Now, about 47 percent of African-Americans live in the Northern states (shaded green).

THE EASTERN UNITED STATES OF AMERICA

US-Canada Border

US State Borders

Confederate//Union States
Border in Civil War

Special Places for
Martin Luther King

Towns/Cities

was already a good preacher. But in Montgomery, he became a *great* preacher. Every Sunday, more and more people came to hear him preach.

In the spring of 1955, Martin finished his studies. He went north to Boston to get his Ph.D. (doctor of philosophy) degree. From then on he was known as "Dr. King" as well as "Reverend King."

That November, Coretta gave birth to their first child, Yolanda (Yoki). Life in Montgomery went on happily for the King family, but times were changing.

17

The need for change

In 1954, the United States Supreme Court decided that the segregation in public schools must stop. Black children and white children were to go to the same schools. Many white people — especially some of those in the Southern states — were very angry about the Supreme Court's decision. By the autumn of 1955, nothing had changed in Montgomery. Black children and white children still went to separate schools.

African-Americans in the South were getting angry, too. They wanted the schools to change. They wanted voting laws to change. According to U.S. law, black people could vote in elections if they were registered like other voters. This means that their names had to be on a special list. Although this is an easy task, many Southern white people tried to keep black people from registering. In Montgomery, for example, only two thousand out of thirty-eight thousand African-Americans were registered.

Most black people were too frightened to demand their rights. If they did, they often lost their jobs. So to stay alive and make some kind of life for their families, many people said nothing. Young Martin Luther King realized that better things would never come for African-Americans if they continued to accept the system of segregation.

The back of the bus

To King, it often seemed that life for African-Americans in the 1950s was the same as it had always been. He often thought of that day on the bus when he and his teacher were made to stand for a white man. The front seats on the Montgomery buses were still only for white people. Black people still had to sit or stand at the back. They could also sit in the middle of the bus, but only if white people did not want the seats.

On the evening of December 1, 1955, a black woman named Rosa Parks got on a bus to go home. Parks worked in a big department store in the center of downtown Montgomery. She had had a hard day at work, and she was very tired.

When Parks got on the bus, it was already crowded. All the seats for blacks were taken, so she found a seat in the middle and sat down. At the next stop, some white people got on. All except one found a seat at the front. One white man remained standing. The rule was that if one white person sat in the middle seats, *all* the black people had to go to the back of the bus. That evening, four blacks were sitting in the middle of the bus. "I need those seats," the driver called. He told Rosa Parks and the other three blacks to go to the back of the bus.

Three of them did as he said. Rosa Parks did not. "Why should one white

Rosa Parks bravely refused to give her bus seat to a white man and was arrested. She was not the kind of person to challenge the law. But that night, she was tired and her feet hurt. The Montgomery Bus Boycott followed her arrest.

man need four seats?" she thought. The driver asked her a second time. "You going to stand up?" he shouted. Again Rosa Parks refused.

The driver called a policeman. When the policeman arrived, he asked Parks why she hadn't stood up. "I didn't think I should have to," she answered. Then she added, "Why do you push us?"

"I don't know," the policeman replied, "but the law is the law, and you are under arrest." Parks was arrested for breaking the city's segregation laws.

Much later, she was asked if she had planned her protest. "No," she said. "I was just tired, and my feet hurt."

Like Rosa Parks, most African-Americans in Montgomery were tired — tired of the way white people insulted them. When the people heard about Rosa Parks' arrest, they were more than tired. They were angry. Here at last was a cause that could unite everyone who hated racism and segregation.

Opposite: King preaches a sermon at Dexter Avenue Baptist Church. King felt that the church could help give African-Americans a feeling that they were real people. He believed that religion should deal with poverty and injustice as well as people's souls. In church the people were free from the unfair white laws.

The boycott plan

After Rosa Parks' arrest, King gathered with some of Montgomery's other black leaders. Included was Ralph Abernathy, another Montgomery minister and one of King's closest friends. Also there was E. D. Nixon, a black man who had fought for black civil rights for many years. He had, in fact, paid Rosa Parks' bail.

People had been angry about the unfair bus system for a long time. Some thought that all black people should stop using the buses, so that the bus company would lose a lot of money. Then perhaps they would have to change their minds. When people do something like this, it is called a "boycott." The time was right to organize a boycott.

Over the weekend, the ministers of all the black churches spread word of the boycott at their services. Meanwhile, a committee prepared and passed out hundreds of leaflets. The leaflets gave news of Rosa Parks' arrest and said:

"Don't ride the buses to work, to town, to school, or anywhere on Monday. If you work, take a cab or share a ride, or walk. Come to a mass meeting, Monday at 7:00 P.M., at Holt Street Baptist Church for further instruction."

The Montgomery Bus Boycott had begun. But how could black people get to work? King and the other black leaders spoke to the city's black-owned taxi companies. They asked the taxi companies to carry passengers for the usual bus fare of ten cents. The taxi companies, which had 210 cars, agreed.

The first day

King got up early on the morning of Monday, December 5, 1955. At 6:00 A.M., he was drinking his coffee in the kitchen

when Coretta called him to the front window. The first bus of the day was driving past their house. Normally, this bus was crammed with people. That day, it was empty. The black people of Montgomery were not using the buses.

Later in the day, Martin drove through the city. He could not believe his eyes. All the buses were empty. The boycott was going better than he had hoped. Many people were walking miles to work rather than taking a bus. Some were driving cars and giving others rides. Some were even riding mules and using horse-drawn carriages.

A black woman during the 1955 bus boycott in Montgomery. The boycott continued for 382 days. During that time, no black person used the city buses. One old woman was offered a ride as she hobbled along one day. She refused it, saying, "I'm not walking for myself. I'm walking for my children and my grandchildren."

About 17,500 black passengers used the buses each day. They made up 75 percent of the passengers. That Monday, no black people rode on the buses at all. As King and the others had hoped, the bus company lost a lot of money.

In the afternoon King, Abernathy, Nixon, and some of the other black leaders met again. They decided to start a new organization, the Montgomery Improvement Association. They elected King president although he was only twenty-six and had lived in the city for only a year. His first job as president was to speak at a meeting that evening.

King's speech

When King arrived at Holt Street Baptist Church, he found a crowd around the building. Inside, the church was already full. Counting a swarm of television and newspaper reporters and photographers, King faced a crowd of about four thousand people. Outside, the police slowly circled the building. They seemed to be expecting trouble.

King nervously stood to speak. He had not had much time to plan what he would say. First, he told the people about Rosa Parks' arrest. Next, he talked about the suffering that segregation had brought to African-Americans. Then he went on to say that they must unite in their fight against racism. He told them

Opposite: Martin at home with Coretta and their four children. King worried that his work was robbing his children of the time a father should spend with them. When he was home, he tried to set aside time to be with them. A picture of Mahatma Gandhi hangs on the wall. King always tried to follow Gandhi's ideas of protest without violence.

24

King's speeches persuaded thousands of people to join in the struggle for equal rights for African-Americans. "There comes a time," he said, "when a moral man can't obey a law which his conscience tells him is unjust. And the important thing is that when he does that, he willingly accepts the consequences."

that they had right and justice on their side. "If we are wrong, the Supreme Court of this nation is wrong. If we are wrong, justice is a lie," he said.

The crowd was completely with King now. They were listening to his every word. He told them about the dangers they would meet. He told them they must not meet violence with violence. Finally, he told them that above all they must not hate their white brothers. They must show love.

King finished speaking and sat down. The crowd cheered. The African-Americans of the South had found their

cause. They had found their leader at last. Martin Luther King had given them courage, hope, and unity. He would help them find justice and dignity. That night, Martin Luther King, Jr., showed the world that he was a great leader.

Three demands

Next, Ralph Abernathy stood up. He read out the three demands of the Montgomery Improvement Association:

1) Bus drivers would treat African-American passengers with courtesy.

2) Passengers would be seated on a first-come, first-serve basis, with black

> *"He could speak better than any man that I've ever heard in expressing to the people their problem and making them see clearly what the situation was and inspiring them to work at it."*
>
> Rufus Lewis,
> a Montgomery businessman

people beginning from the back and white people from the front.

3) The bus company must hire black drivers on routes that went through black areas.

King asked the crowd to stand if they agreed with these demands. The whole crowd stood.

In the civil rights movement, many white people joined African-Americans in their fight. Martin told his followers again and again that they must not be bitter. When the bus boycott was over, he told the crowd: "We must take this not as victory over the white man but as a victory for justice and democracy."

The first rainy day

Montgomery's mayor, W. A. Gayle, met with King and the other black leaders. It was clear that he did not intend to stop segregation on the buses. He said, "Come the first rainy day and all the Negroes will be back on the buses!"

But he was wrong.

The police and the mayor soon stopped the ten-cent taxi system, but the Montgomery Improvement Association began a car pool. Over three hundred people gave their cars with themselves as drivers. Soon the car pool was doing as much business as the bus company had done. Many black people still walked to work; they wanted people to see their protest. The Montgomery Improvement Association hoped that the newspapers, radio, and television would tell the world about their protest. And they did.

The whites fight back

Racist white people in Montgomery grew more angry about the newspaper and television reports of the boycott. The world was laughing at them. The mayor and the police chief, two of the most powerful men in Montgomery, soon announced that they would be hard on the black protesters from now on.

The police began stopping car-pool drivers for any reason or none at all. One day, King was stopped for speeding. He was arrested and spent a few hours in the city jail before he was let out on bail. This was the first of his many visits to jail during his time as a civil rights leader.

Meeting hatred with love

Some white organizations, including the Ku Klux Klan, took the law into their

"If we don't stop helping these African flesh eaters, we will soon wake up and find Reverend King in the White House."

From a leaflet sent by white segregationists

A member of the Ku Klux Klan. During the bus boycott, King got a letter that said, "If you allow the niggers to go back on the buses and sit in the front seats, we're going to burn down fifty houses in one night, including yours."

Above: Segregationists worked hard to stop blacks from getting equal rights.

Below: A sign posted by the Klan "welcomes" visitors.

own hands. By January 1956, King and his family were getting thirty to forty hate letters every day. In the letters, many of the writers threatened to kill Martin and Coretta.

Four days after King's first arrest, the threats became real. Martin was speaking at a meeting when he heard that his house had been bombed. He rushed home; Coretta and the baby were safe. Someone had thrown a bomb onto the front porch. The explosion had ripped the porch apart and shattered the windows. Amazingly, no one was hurt.

A crowd of black people gathered outside the house. They were angry that someone had attacked the Kings. The police, led by the police chief and the mayor, came too. The police tried to send the crowd home, but the crowd would not listen. King was worried. The crowd was becoming dangerous. He saw that many people were carrying knives, stones, and broken bottles. He went out and spoke to them at once.

"My wife and baby are all right," he said. "I want you all to go home. . . . We cannot solve this problem through . . . violence. We must meet hatred with love. Remember, if I am stopped, this movement will not stop because God is with this movement."

The dangerous moment had passed. The crowd began to go home.

Above: Protest marches were met with anger and hatred. When King led his people through the city, bystanders screamed "Hate! Hate! Hate!"

Left: Segregationists lined the pavements during marches. They often carried signs with slogans such as "Segregation forever!" or "Go home to Africa!"

31

Above: Coretta Scott King spends a moment with her youngest daughter, Bunny.

Right: Coretta at the piano with Bunny, Marty, and Yoki.

Coretta and Martin march together. Coretta stood by Martin through the years of danger. She kept their family close and loving although Martin was often away from home. Coretta said of her husband, "He was a good man — such a very good man." She says he was a truly humble man who never felt he deserved his fame.

The boycott continues

All through the early months of 1956, the city's black community continued its boycott. The people did not use buses; they walked. The mayor and many of the whites in the city tried hard to break the boycott. They found an old Alabama law which said that boycotts were illegal. Under that law, King and eighty-eight other people were arrested. King was the first person to be found guilty under that law. His lawyers immediately took the case to a higher court. King had to wait many months for a result.

Meanwhile, another case was being heard in a federal court. In that case, the Montgomery Improvement Association was fighting against bus segregation.

"There was never a moment when we were not united in our love and dedication, never a moment that I wanted to be anything but the wife of Martin Luther King."
Coretta Scott King, in
My Life with
Martin Luther King

They believed it was against the Constitution. In June, the court agreed. The mayor then took the case on to the Supreme Court.

Meanwhile, in November 1956, the city ruled that carpooling was illegal. Was this to be the end of the boycott? Was this the end of all their hopes?

The Supreme Court decides

On November 13, King was in court in Montgomery. He was listening to the case against the car pool. Suddenly, a newspaper reporter gave him a piece of paper. The paper was a telegram from the United States Supreme Court in Washington. The Supreme Court had ruled that segregation on Alabama's buses was illegal. The Montgomery Improvement Association had won.

King knew that white segregationists would not accept the court's decision quietly. He was right. The Ku Klux Klan marched through the streets in protest. But now, when the Klan marched, the African-Americans did not run away. This time, they stayed and watched. They had found new courage.

More violence followed. One night bombs exploded in four black churches and at the homes of two black ministers. Soon after that, another bomb was thrown at the Kings' house. Luckily, it did not explode.

When segregation on the buses finally ended on December 21, 1956, King was the first black passenger. With him was Rosa Parks, the woman who had started it all. The leaders, black and white, who had fought so long to end segregation were with him, too.

As King got on the bus, the white driver said, "I believe you are the Reverend King, aren't you?"

"Yes, I am," Martin answered.

"We're glad to have you with us this morning," the driver said.

"We are on the move now," said King in one speech. "Like an idea whose time has come, not even the marching of mighty armies can stop us. We're moving to the land of freedom." "Freedom" became the word on the lips of all protesters in the civil rights movement.

The civil rights movement grows

Montgomery was only the beginning. It gave courage and hope to African-

Above: Martin with his younger son, Dexter Scott.

Right: Martin with his first son, Martin Luther King III (Marty).

"My husband often told the children that if a man had nothing that was worth dying for, then he was not fit to live. He said also that it's not how long you live, but how well you live."

Coretta Scott King, in
My Life with
Martin Luther King

Americans all over the Southern states. Protests and boycotts began in many places. But to be successful, the black community had to be united. In January 1957, the Southern Christian Leadership Conference (SCLC) was started to advise and help unite the community. Martin Luther King became its president.

King was now clearly the leader of the black civil rights movement. As the leader, he wanted to do as much as he

Above: King playing baseball with Marty.

Left: King spends a happy moment in the garden with Bunny, his youngest daughter. Although he was busy with meetings and speeches, King tried to find time to play and laugh with his children.

could to help the movement. His life grew busier each day. Much of his time was spent making speeches. He was asked to speak at meetings all over the country. During 1957 and 1958, he made a total of 208 speeches.

King worked hard and was often tired. His time at home with Coretta, Yolanda, and their new baby son was very short. Coretta kept the family loving and close, but it was a difficult time for Martin. He

37

felt he had to push on. He had to tell the world about the problems of African-Americans in the South.

On September 10, 1958, King came face to face with the hatred that his work had brought him. He was in a bookshop in New York. He was signing copies of his book, *Stride Toward Freedom*, for customers. A middle-aged black woman came up to him. "Are you Martin Luther King?" she asked.

"Yes, I am," he answered. With that, the woman stabbed King with a letter opener. It was found out later that King's attacker was insane.

King was rushed to a hospital. The knife was still in his body. He had to have surgery to have it removed. A doctor said later that if he had sneezed or coughed, he would have died.

At the end of 1959, King moved to Atlanta. He became co-minister, with his father, of the Ebenezer Baptist Church. This move would give him more time for his work as president of the SCLC.

The student movement

Segregation on the buses had been only one problem for African-Americans in the South. In 1960, a black student was refused service at a bus station restaurant in North Carolina. The student and two of his friends protested. They followed King's ideas of nonviolence carefully.

"The greatness of this period was that we armed ourselves with dignity and self-respect. The greatness of this period was that we straightened our backs up. And a man can't ride your back unless it's bent."

Martin Luther King, Jr.

Day after day, they went to the restaurant and sat down. Each day, more students joined them. They were never served. Newspapers began to report the story. Sit-ins began all over the South, in restaurants, shops, theaters, libraries — anywhere that black people were not served. Students started the Student Nonviolent Coordinating Committee (SNCC) to help each other.

King helped the SNCC. He often joined them at their sit-ins. During one sit-in at Atlanta in June 1960, he and seventy-five other people were arrested. Everyone except King was set free after a few days. When his case came to court, King was found guilty. He was given four months of hard labor in the state prison. It was a very heavy sentence.

The next morning, Coretta received a telephone call from Senator John F. Kennedy. Kennedy was the Democratic candidate in the presidential election that autumn. He had heard about Martin's sentence. He wanted to help. Coretta thanked him. In the meantime, Robert Kennedy, who was John's brother and a lawyer, spoke to the judge in King's case. He asked that King be released on bail. The judge agreed. Martin was free again.

The Freedom Riders

The sit-ins worked well. Many restaurants and big stores began to serve

"The nonviolent approach does not immediately change the heart of the oppressor. It first does something to the hearts and souls of those committed to it. It gives them new self-respect; it calls up resources of strength and courage that they did not know they had. Finally it reaches the opponent and so stirs his conscience that reconciliation becomes a reality."

Martin Luther King, Jr.

The first Freedom Riders' bus after it was attacked in Anniston, Alabama. A white gang smashed the bus, set it on fire, and beat the passengers. Nine white men were later caught, but they were not punished.

African-Americans in the early 1960s. But there was still segregation to be fought in many other places. In the summer of 1961, black and white students from the North tried a new kind of protest. They wanted to end segregation on the buses that traveled across state lines as well as those that traveled in the cities. Called the "Freedom Riders," they traveled south by bus, holding sit-ins at restaurants and bus stations along the way.

For ten days, they did not meet any trouble. But white segregationists in the South were very angry. When the first Freedom Riders reached Alabama, members of the Ku Klux Klan attacked the bus. The Klansmen beat the students, nearly killing some of them. The students did not fight back. Then the Klansmen set fire to the bus.

King was shocked by the violence of the Klansmen. He decided to help the students. On May 21, he spoke at a meeting at the First Baptist Church in Montgomery. He asked people to help the Freedom Riders. A group of white segregationists gathered outside the church. First, they set fire to some cars. Suddenly stones shattered the church windows. Gas bombs followed. With the mob outside and fire inside, the people in the church were trapped.

But the law came to the people's aid. National Guard soldiers arrived in time to save all the people inside the church.

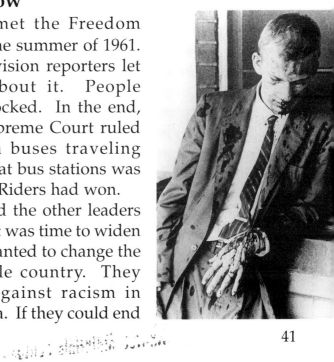

When the Freedom Riders reached Montgomery, James Zwerg, a student from Wisconsin, was badly beaten. He made no attempt to fight back. No white ambulances would help the Freedom Riders, so Zwerg had to wait for a black ambulance to come.

The end of Jim Crow

The violence that met the Freedom Riders grew during the summer of 1961. Newspaper and television reporters let the world know about it. People everywhere were shocked. In the end, the United States Supreme Court ruled that segregation on buses traveling across state lines and at bus stations was illegal. The Freedom Riders had won.

After this, King and the other leaders of the SCLC decided it was time to widen their protest. They wanted to change the attitude of the whole country. They began their fight against racism in Birmingham, Alabama. If they could end racism in the city of Birmingham, maybe they could end it throughout the entire United States.

The sit-ins, boycotts, and protest marches began in April 1963. The protesters wanted the city to end segregation and to give black people equality with white people at work.

One of the leaders of the white segregationists was Eugene "Bull" Connor. He was the city's police commissioner. He said that "blood would run in the streets of Birmingham" before he would agree to desegregation. To him, all African-Americans were no more than "dirty niggers."

"Letter from Birmingham Jail"

During the first big protest march on April 12, King was arrested. He was taken to the Birmingham jail. While he sat in jail, some white ministers wrote to the Birmingham newspaper. They called King an outsider. They said he had no right to be in Birmingham. They asked the city's black people to stop the protest.

King was hurt by the ministers' letter. But he could not answer them. He had no paper in jail, and the police would not give him any. In desperation, King used any paper he could — bags, toilet paper, the edges of newspapers. On them, he wrote his beliefs. This document is now known as the "Letter from Birmingham

Opposite: King sits in Birmingham's jail. He was arrested, along with nine hundred others, for marching and singing freedom songs. The jails were so full that they couldn't hold everyone. For eight days, King was alone. During that time, he wrote his "Letter from Birmingham Jail." This letter soon appeared in newspapers, magazines, and leaflets all over the United States.

Jail." It is one of the most important writings of the civil rights movement in the United States.

The white ministers had called King an outsider. He wrote, "I am in Birmingham because injustice is here." He said injustice is a universal thing that has nothing to do with insiders or outsiders. He also said that nonviolent protests were necessary; they made people see that something was wrong. He did not think it was the wrong time for protests. He said, "For years now I have heard the word 'Wait! . . .' This 'Wait' has almost always meant 'never.'"

After eight days, King was freed. John F. Kennedy, now president, had helped again. He had asked Birmingham's police chief to let King see a lawyer.

The protest marches continued. But the black community was losing heart. So many people had been arrested. King and the other black leaders decided to ask the students for their help. Surprisingly, even small schoolchildren asked to join the protest. The leaders worried about the danger. But King knew that the future of the children was at stake. So they let the children march.

On May 2, 1963, one thousand children joined the march through the city from the Sixteenth Street Baptist Church. "We want freedom!" they shouted. That day, the police arrested

eight hundred people. Hundreds of those arrested were children. The police used school buses to take them to jail.

The next day, more children and students marched through the city. The police told them to stop, but they did not. "Let them have it!" Bull Connor shouted.

The Birmingham firemen turned on their hoses. Great jets of water hit the protesters. The water's force toppled children like pieces of paper. Many people were hurt. The protesters began fighting with the police. Then the police turned their dogs on the protesters. Bull Connor laughed and shouted, "Look at those niggers run!"

All through the march, the television cameras were working. The next day, people all over the United States saw the terrible pictures: the smiling policemen, the angry dogs, the frightened children.

Victory for nonviolent protest

Still the black community in Birmingham did not stop their protest. Every day, the people went out into the streets. Every day, they met the violent police. Every day, they sang their songs of freedom.

And then — on May 5, 1963 — something wonderful happened.

Black ministers were leading a protest march to the Birmingham jail when they met a line of policemen. The marchers went down on their knees and prayed for a few minutes. Then they stood up and walked forward.

Connor was there.

"Turn on the hoses!" he shouted to his firemen. "Turn on the hoses!"

But the policemen and the firemen did not move. They looked at the quiet faces of the marchers, and then they moved back. They let the marchers go through. Connor was very, very angry. But he could do nothing.

King's belief in the goodness of all people was right. Nonviolent protest had won in Birmingham. But the cost had been great. Three thousand people had been arrested during the protests.

Bull Connor and Abe Lincoln

Birmingham's businessmen finally agreed to give African-Americans equality with whites at work. The city started a special group to solve problems between black and white communities. Jailed protesters were freed.

More important, the federal laws on civil rights were changed. President Kennedy put forward a new civil rights bill to the United States Congress.

Kennedy said later that "Bull Connor has done as much for civil rights as Abraham Lincoln!" Connor had made many Americans think about justice for the black community for the first time. But Connor had not done much good for himself. Shortly after all this, he lost his job as police commissioner.

During the protest marches, many young marchers wore an equality sign on their foreheads. This showed that they believed in the cause of African-American civil rights.

The 1963 March on Washington

Later that summer, a march was planned. It took place on August 28, 1963, in Washington, D.C. That day, over 250 thousand people walked down Pennsylvania Avenue to the Lincoln Memorial. When Martin and Coretta arrived, they were stunned. They had hoped for 100 thousand people. But 250 thousand was unbelievable. About half of the marchers were black people, and half were white people. It showed that white people were starting to understand African-Americans' problems.

One hundred years earlier, during the Civil War, the famous Emancipation Proclamation had announced the end of slavery. Many marchers carried signs which said, "We seek the freedom in 1963 promised in 1863!"

King had planned his speech carefully. He wanted his words to change people's hearts. He recalled the Emancipation Proclamation and the equality it had promised years earlier. Black people still did not have that equality! The crowd cheered King. They knew he spoke *for* them as well as *to* them.

"I have a dream"

Moved by their support, King put away his notes and spoke from his heart. And from his heart came one of the greatest

speeches in American history, his "I Have a Dream" speech.

King spoke of his hopes for his children, for all children, for his nation: "One day, this nation will rise up and live out the true meaning of its creed: 'We

King speaks from the steps of the Lincoln Memorial in Washington, D.C. He made the greatest speech of his life on that day. His "I Have a Dream" speech has since become part of history.

hold these truths to be self-evident: that all men are created equal. . . .'

"I have a dream that one day . . . the sons of former slaves and the sons of former slave owners will be able to sit . . . together at the table of brotherhood.

"I have a dream that my four little children will one day live in a nation where they will be judged not by the color of their skin, but by the content of their character. . . .

"When we allow freedom to ring . . . from every village and hamlet, from every state and every city, we will be able to speed up that day when all of God's children, black men and white men, Jews and Gentiles, Protestants and Catholics, will be able to join hands and sing in the words of the old Negro spiritual, 'Free at last! Free at last! Thank God Almighty, we are free at last!'"

The crowd exploded. He had again given a voice to the civil rights movement in America. The newspapers that day called King the "president of Black America." August 28, 1963, had been a great day in Martin Luther King's life and in the history of America.

A hope too soon

When King spoke to the crowds in Washington that day, he and many other Americans hoped that the victory of Birmingham could happen all over the country. But that hope came too soon. A few weeks later, on September 15, a bomb exploded at the Sixteenth Street Baptist Church in Birmingham. Four young girls were killed and twenty-one people were badly hurt.

Two months later, on Friday, November 22, 1963, President Kennedy was assassinated in Dallas, Texas. He was shot as he and his wife, Jacqueline, were being driven through the streets. The president who had done so much for the cause of civil rights was dead. King worried what the future would bring.

Vice President Lyndon B. Johnson now became president. Johnson came from the South. What would he do for the civil rights movement? Johnson surprised King. Five days after Kennedy's assassination, Johnson asked Congress to work on a new civil rights bill. The bill became law on July 2, 1964. President Johnson did a lot for the African-American cause.

In October 1964, King went to Norway to receive the Nobel Peace Prize. It was a great moment in his life. At thirty-five, he was the youngest man to win the prize. He gave the prize money to U.S. civil rights organizations.

Selma, Alabama

Back home in America, there were still great problems. One of the most difficult

"Few can explain the extraordinary King mystique. Yet he has an indescribable capacity for empathy that is the touchstone of leadership. By deed and by preachment, he has stirred in his people a Christian forbearance that nourishes hope and smothers injustice."
Time, *January 3, 1964, on naming King its "Man of the Year" for 1963*

problems was that thousands of black people were still not registered to vote in elections. King and the other civil rights leaders decided that they must change this. They began their work in Selma, Alabama, where only 150 out of 15,000 African-Americans were registered.

On January 18, 1965, King led four hundred black people to register in Selma. They were told that the office was closed. They could not register. On February 1, King and a large group of black people tried again to register in Selma. They were all arrested.

When he was set free, King decided that the people must go to Montgomery and appeal to Governor George Wallace. A march from Selma to Montgomery was planned for Sunday, March 7. Five hundred people began the march from Selma, but just outside the town, the march was stopped by state policemen. The marchers were violently attacked. The police beat them. Seventeen people were hurt. For a long time, the police did not let doctors help them.

Martin planned a second march for Tuesday, March 9. This time, he had help from religious leaders from all over America. But this second march was stopped in the same place by local authorities. Again, the authorities turned the marchers back. But this time, no one was hurt.

For the first time, a black candidate runs in an election in Greene County, Alabama.

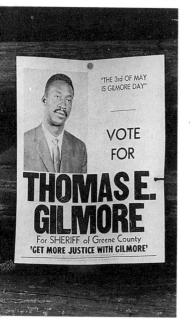

"THE 3rd OF MAY IS GILMORE DAY"

VOTE FOR

THOMAS E. GILMORE

For SHERIFF of Greene County

'GET MORE JUSTICE WITH GILMORE'

Soon afterward, three white ministers from Boston who had come to help the civil rights movement in Selma were attacked by the Ku Klux Klan. One of them was killed. All of America was shocked again by the violence of the white segregationists in the South.

On Monday, March 15, President Johnson spoke to Congress. He asked them to vote on a new voting rights bill the next Wednesday. He realized that something had to be done quickly to stop the violence in Selma.

That Wednesday, the ban was lifted on the march from Selma to Montgomery. The march finally took place on March 21. This time, four thousand federal troops guarded the marchers. The march

A black woman votes in an election for the first time. The Civil Rights Act of 1964 made this possible. On July 2, 1964, President Johnson signed the bill. On television he said that "those who are equal before God should now be equal in the polling booths, in classrooms, in the factories, and in hotels, restaurants, movie theaters, and other places that provide services to the public."

Above: State troopers carrying sticks stopped people on the first Selma-to-Montgomery march. The policemen hurt seventeen people.

Opposite, below: The second march from Selma to Montgomery was held March 9. This march was also stopped just outside Selma. The people prayed and turned back. This time, no one was hurt.

took five days, and at the end, there were thirty thousand people on the road.

Because of the events at Selma, the Voting Rights Act of 1965 became law. At last, African-Americans could vote in their country's elections without fear. And the federal government had the power to make the states follow the law.

Up North

Life for African-Americans away from the Southern states was not perfect either. In many parts of Northern cities

where black people lived, people were poor. Many had no jobs.

By the mid-1960s, many African-Americans no longer saw nonviolence as the answer to their problems. The way of nonviolent protest was too slow. They could not wait forever. The Black Power movement, started by leaders like Stokely Carmichael, grew quickly. Carmichael believed that African-Americans "must get power at any cost."

As this movement grew, terrible rioting broke out. Riots erupted in

Stokely Carmichael, a friend of King's, was one of many African-Americans who, by the mid-1960s, did not agree with Martin's ideas about nonviolent protest. He was the first person to use the term "Black Power."

Chicago, Los Angeles, and cities all over the country. King did not agree with the Black Power movement. He continued to preach his ideas of nonviolence.

The promised land

In April 1968, he went to Memphis, Tennessee. The city's black garbage collectors were paid less than the white garbage collectors. The black garbage collectors wanted pay and rights equal to those of the whites.

On April 3, King's plane from Atlanta was delayed. Someone had told the airline that a bomb had been hidden on the plane. There was no bomb, but King was late for his meeting in Memphis. He was tired and nervous when he arrived. He told those at the meeting what had happened. He talked about the dangers that he and his family had to live with.

"Like anybody," he said, "I would like to live a long life. But I am not concerned about that now. I just want to do God's will. And he's allowed me to go up to the mountain. And I've looked over and I've seen the promised land. I may not get there with you. But I want you to know tonight that we, as a people, will get to the promised land."

The next day, King worked in his hotel room with friends. They planned the next steps in the Memphis protest. King again said there must be no violence. In

the evening, Ralph Abernathy and King went out on the balcony of King's room. Suddenly, there was the sound of a gunshot. King fell to the ground, a bullet in his neck. His friends rushed him to a hospital, but an hour later he was dead.

In this photo, federal troops guard the protesters during a march through Memphis, Tennessee. The marchers were black garbage collectors who wanted pay and rights equal to those of the white garbage collectors.

The death of nonviolence?

Martin Luther King's death was a terrible shock to people all over the world. For many African-Americans, he had been their only hope. Now he was gone.

All his life he had tried to follow the way of nonviolence. After his death, a great wave of riots swept over the country. Thirty-nine people died, and hundreds more were hurt.

REV. MARTIN LUTHER KING JR.
1929 ——— 1968
"FREE AT LAST, FREE AT LAST,
THANK GOD ALMIGHTY I'M FREE AT LAST."

Above: People all over the world were shocked by Martin Luther King's death.

Opposite: Coretta Scott King at her husband's funeral.

"The day that Negro people . . . are truly free, on the day when want is abolished, on the day wars are no more, on that day I know my husband will rest in . . . peace."
Coretta Scott King, in
My Life with
Martin Luther King

Free at last

Martin Luther King had not had a long life. He was only thirty-nine when he died. But his life had changed the lives of thousands of African-Americans.

King's funeral was held at the Ebenezer Baptist Church in Atlanta, where he had preached his first sermon. His father led the service. Over 100 thousand people gathered to mourn the death of this great leader. They flowed behind the wagon, pulled by two mules, that carried King's coffin to the grave.

As the mule wagon reminded black people of their beginnings, so did the words on King's gravestone. King had used the words, which came from a great black song, in his speech in Washington in 1963: "Free at last. Free at last. Thank God Almighty, I'm free at last."

To find out more . . .

Organizations

The groups listed below are concerned about many of the issues that you have read about in this biography. If you would like to know more about these issues, write to the groups at the addresses below. When you write, be sure to tell them exactly what you would like to know. Also include your name, address, and age.

Association for the Study of Afro-American Life and History
1401 Fourteenth Street NW
Washington, DC 20005

National Association for the Advancement of Colored People
(NAACP)
4805 Mount Hope Drive
Baltimore, MD 21215

National Alliance of Black School Educators
2816 Georgia Avenue NW
Washington, DC 20001

Southern Christian Leadership Conference
334 Auburn Avenue NE
Atlanta, GA 30312

Also, the National Association for the Advancement of Colored People (NAACP) and the National Urban League may have local chapters in your city. If you would like to reach these groups, call or write to them at the addresses listed in your telephone book.

Books

The books listed on the next page will give you more information about civil rights and the Reverend Martin Luther King, Jr. Check your local library or bookstore to see if they have them or if someone there can order them for you.

60

About Martin Luther King Day. Fox (Enslow Publications)

I Have a Dream: The Story of Martin Luther King. Davidson
   (Scholastic)

Marching to Freedom: The Story of Martin Luther King, Jr.
   Milton (Dell)

Martin Luther King. Bains (Troll Associates)

Martin Luther King Day. Lowery (Carolrhoda Books)

Martin Luther King, Jr. Hunter (Franklin Watts)

Martin Luther King, Jr. Ottenheimer (Wanderer Books)

Martin Luther King, Jr.: Free at Last. Adler (Holiday)

Martin Luther King, Jr.: A Man to Remember. McKissack
   (Childrens Press)

Martin Luther King: The Peaceful Warrior. Clayton (Archway)

Martin Luther King, Jr.: The Story of a Dream. Behrens
   (Childrens Press)

Martin Luther King, Jr.: Young Man with a Dream. Millender
   (Macmillan)

Also, America's Public Broadcasting System has produced an impressive series about the history of the civil rights movement called "Eyes on the Prize." Videocassettes of this series are available for viewing free from many public libraries. Call or visit your library to see if you may borrow the cassettes.

List of new words

abolish
   To stop, or do away with, something such as regulations or
   circumstances that are no longer wanted.

appeal
   A request to reconsider a dispute. When a court has decided
   that a person is guilty of a crime, that person can appeal to a
   higher court to change the first court's decision.

arrest
   To capture and hold a person who is suspected of breaking a

law. Normally, in most states, only local, county, or state police have the authority to arrest people.

assassination

The murder of an important person. This word is also used to refer to damaging gossip that is meant to hurt a person; it destroys the person's character in the eyes of others.

bail

Money paid by some people who have been arrested. Bail is paid by these people so they do not have to wait in jail until their trial is scheduled in court. People out on bail have to promise to appear in court at a later date. If they do not appear in court on that date, the court keeps the money.

ban

To prohibit or to announce that something must not take place; sometimes people are banned from entering certain places.

bill

An idea introduced into Congress or a state legislature. If lawmakers agree that the bill is important, they make it a law.

boycott

To refuse to use or buy a certain product or to buy from a certain business. People usually boycott businesses when they want to force them to behave in a certain way.

candidate

A person who is being considered for a position, usually for a governmental office.

car pool

A system set up so people who own cars can give rides to people who do not own cars. In some car pools, car owners may simply take turns giving one another rides to save on gas.

civil disobedience

Peacefully breaking a law you think is wrong. This is usually done so that the lawbreaker can gain public attention and convince others that the law is wrong. People who commit acts of civil disobedience know that they may be punished. But they accept this as the price they pay to achieve their goals.

civil rights

The right to freedom and equal treatment in a country, as these they would be spelled out by laws.

Congress

The group of elected men and women who make the laws in the federal government of the United States.

court

A place where cases are tried. Cases are tried before a judge, or sometimes before both a judge and a jury.

desegregate

To make it possible for people of all races to be together in schools, neighborhoods, churches, restaurants, theaters, and anyplace else.

federal

The type of government that has a central government over-seeing certain national activities and policies. All the states in the nation agree to unify and be governed by that government. But the states still govern themselves on some matters.

government

A system that manages the business of a city (or other local area), county, state, or nation.

governor

In the United States, the person who heads a state government.

guilty
  Responsible for doing something against the law. The
  court system determines if a person is guilty or not guilty.

hard labor
  Difficult physical work done by convicted criminals as a
  punishment. Hard labor was not unusual as punishment in
  many countries in the past. But it is not common now in
  democratic countries.

illegal
  Against the law of a city (or other local area), county, state,
  or nation.

judge
  A person who hears cases in court and decides whether a
  person is guilty or not guilty. Sometimes a jury, rather than a
  judge, makes that decision. In those cases, the judge often
  decides the punishment.

justice
  That which is right and fair. When everyone is treated fairly,
  under equal rules, there is justice.

mayor
  The top official in a city or town.

minister
  In many faiths, a preacher or member of the clergy.

ordain
  To perform a ceremony that makes a person a priest, minister,
  rabbi, or other member of the clergy.

Ph.D.
  Abbreviation for a degree given by a college or university. The

initials stand for *Philosophiae Doctor*. This is Latin for "Doctor of Philosophy."

preach
To deliver a sermon, usually in a church.

protest
To speak out strongly against something illegal or wrong.

punish
To make someone suffer for doing something wrong.

racism
The belief that one race or group of people is better than another. In this book, the racism appears in those white people who think that they are superior to black people.

register
To put your name on a list.

riot
An unruly free-for-all during which people behave violently and break the law.

segregate
To separate people. Years ago, in many areas of the United States, black people and white people were kept separate by law.

sentence
The punishment given to a person who has been found guilty in a court.

sermon
A speech on a religious idea or theme. It is usually given in a church.

sit-in
An event that consists of sitting down in offices, restaurants, streets, or other places as a way of getting public attention and protesting something. Many protesters at sit-ins must be carried away by the local police.

slavery
The system that enables one person to own another.

Supreme Court
The highest court in the United States.

Important dates

1929   **January 15** — Martin Luther King, Jr., is born in Atlanta, Georgia.

1948   King is ordained as a Baptist minister. He goes to Crozer Theological Seminary, in Chester, Pennsylvania.

1953   King marries Coretta Scott in Marion, Alabama.

1954   King becomes minister of Dexter Avenue Baptist Church, Montgomery, Alabama.
The U.S. Supreme Court decides in *Brown* vs. *Topeka Board of Education* that public schools must be integrated.

1955   King gets his Ph.D. in theology from Boston University.
December 1 — Rosa Parks is arrested.
December 5 — The Montgomery Bus Boycott begins.

1956   **January 26** — King is jailed for the first time, when officials accuse him of speeding.
February 21 — King and eighty-eight others are jailed for violating archaic "anti-boycott" laws.
June 4 — A federal court decides that segregation on the buses in Montgomery is illegal.

November 13 — The Supreme Court agrees with the federal court's decision.

December 21 — Buses in Montgomery are desegregated for the first time.

1960   The first sit-in protest is held at a restaurant in Greensboro, North Carolina.

The Student Nonviolent Coordinating Committee (SNCC) is started.

King is jailed after a sit-in in Atlanta.

1961   The first Freedom Riders try to stop segregation on buses crossing state lines and in restaurants. In Anniston, Alabama, they are attacked, and their bus is burned.

1963   Martin writes his "Letter from a Birmingham Jail" after his arrest during the protests in that city.

"Bull" Connor, the Birmingham police chief, orders his men to use fire hoses and police dogs against the marchers.

August 28 — The "March on Washington" attracts 250 thousand supporters of civil rights. King makes his "I Have a Dream" speech on the steps of the Lincoln Memorial.

1965   **March 7** — People on a march from Selma to Montgomery, Alabama, are violently attacked by the state police.

1966   Twenty-three people are killed, and 725 are badly hurt during riots in Newark, New Jersey. Forty-three people are killed, and 324 are badly hurt during the worst riots of the century in Detroit, Michigan.

1968   **April 3** — Martin makes his speech about the "Promised Land" in Memphis, Tennessee.

April 4 — Martin, standing on the balcony of his motel in Memphis, Tennessee, is assassinated by a gunman.

Index

Abernathy, Ralph 20, 24, 27, 56
anti-boycott law 33

Birmingham jail 42, 43, 44
   black clergymen's march on 46;
   King's letter from 42, 44
"Black Power" movement 54-55, 56

Carmichael, Stokley 54, 55, 56
CITIES: Atlanta, Georgia 10, 11, 12, 13,
   38, 39, 56, 57, 58; Birmingham,
   Alabama 41, 42, 43, 44, 45, 46, 47,
   50; Boston, Massachusetts 15, 16,
   52; Memphis, Tennessee 55, 56, 57;
   Montgomery, Alabama 15, 16, 17,
   18, 19, 20, 22, 23, 28, 29, 30, 34, 35,
   41, 52, 53, 54; New York, New York
   38; Selma, Alabama 51, 52, 53, 54
civil rights 47, 51
   bills 47, 51, 53; movement 20, 28,
   35, 36, 42, 48, 49, 50, 51, 54
Civil War 6, 7, 16, 17, 47
Connor, Eugene ("Bull") 42, 44, 45,
   46, 47

Dexter Avenue Baptist Church 15, 16,
   20, 21

Ebenezer Baptist Church 10, 13, 38, 57
Emancipation Proclamation 6, 48

Freedom Riders 39, 40, 41

Gandhi, Mahatma 12, 15, 24, 25

"Jim Crow" 7, 41
Johnson, Lyndon B. 51, 52, 53

Kennedy, John F. 39, 44, 47, 50-51
Kennedy, Robert 39
King, Coretta Scott 15, 16, 17, 22, 24,
   25, 29, 30, 32, 33, 36, 37, 39, 47, 58
King, Martin Luther, Jr.

arrests of 29, 33, 39, 42-43, 52; birth
   of 10; childhood of 10-12; death of
   56; family of 10; as leader of march
   on Washington, D.C. 47-48; letters
   and speeches of 42, 44, 48-50;
   marriage of 15; as minister 13-14,
   15-16, 20, 21, 26, 27; as parent 17,
   24, 25, 32, 36-37; as president of
   Southern Christian Leadership
   Conference 36; stabbing of 38; wins
   Nobel Peace Prize 51
King, Martin Luther, Sr. 10, 12, 38, 57
Ku Klux Klan (KKK) 7-10, 11, 29, 30,
   34, 40, 41, 52

Lincoln, Abraham 47
Lincoln Memorial 47, 50

Montgomery Improvement
   Association 24, 27-28, 29, 33, 34

Parks, Rosa 19-20, 22, 24, 34

racism 7, 8, 10, 11, 12, 16, 20, 24, 29, 41

segregation 7, 8, 10, 11, 12, 16, 17, 18,
   20, 24, 28, 38, 39, 40, 41, 42, 44; on
   buses 11, 12, 18-19, 20, 33, 34-35,
   40, 41; in restaurants 7, 38, 39, 40;
   in schools 11, 17, 18; sit-ins 38-39,
   40, 42
slavery 4, 5, 6, 7, 48, 50
Southern Christian Leadership
   Conference (SCLC) 36, 38, 41
Student Nonviolent Coordinating
   Committee (SNCC) 39

U.S. Supreme Court 17, 24, 33, 34, 41

Voting Rights Act 53

Wallace, George 52
War Between the States (*see* Civil War)